Chakra Sun Signs

Santina Cross

Contents

Preface. A Fool's Journey

A Brief History on the Author's Discovery of Chakra Sun Signs

This book is not based on an overnight discovery, but rather on a long journey of stumbling upon Spirit's clues. In hindsight, I can look back on my life and see how Spirit has always been with me. Still, my true spiritual journey began one morning in the spring of 1996. That day, I woke up crying with dread. I had dreamed my friend had fallen after climbing a mountain without gear. In my dream, I watched an ambulance come and take her away. This was the most authentic dream I had ever had. I woke not knowing if my friend was alive.

Still crying, I grabbed the phone. I needed to hear my friend's voice to know she was ok. To my relief, she answered. She was rushing out the door to university, but took the time to laugh and reassure me before hanging up. But later that day, on her way home from school, my friend was in an accident. A car from the opposite lane crossed the median line and drove straight into her vehicle. When I first got the news, I was in shock. All I knew was she had been in a bad accident, and rushed to the hospital by ambulance. Fortunately, while my dear friend was seriously injured, she eventually made a full recovery. However, we never forgot that dream.

Over the months that followed, I had several other minor dreams about people that came true. Since childhood, I had always had intense dreams; however, never any like these. While the facts always differed in my dreams, the outcomes were spot on with reality. These unexplained connections between my dreams and my life aroused my curiosity. I began to realize for the first time that there might be more to the world than what I'd been taught, or what I could see.

That Christmas, I asked for a Tarot deck in the family gift exchange, and my favourite aunt gave me my first set of Tarot cards. While I had no previous experience with tools of divination, I hoped that I would be able to use the cards to tap into the same higher consciousness that was guiding my dreams.

Starting with the facts, I learned that the Tarot deck is made up of 78 cards. The pack is then divided between the 56 Minor Arcana and the 22 Major Arcana. The Minor Arcana are based on a regular deck of cards, with the addition of Pages in the royalty cards of Knights, Queens, and Kings. These are said to indicate everyday occurrences, people, and relationships in our lives. The Major Arcana (0-21) tells the story of the FOOL (0), who represents ourselves on our continuing 21-step journey to enlightenment, or THE WORLD (21). These cards are said to represent the major occurrences in our lives and show where we may be positioned on our own paths.

All of the cards are richly coded in meaning, and hold symbols of numerology, archetypes, colours, elements, and astrology. "Arcana" literally means "secret" in Latin, and the Tarot holds them all, both major and minor. These secrets come together to tell a story. In Tarot we look for clues in the cards to tell us what's going on. I knew that if I were going to become a guide to people's personal stories, I'd have to learn as much about these secrets as I could.

As I worked with the cards, the most obvious clue to me was numerology. Each number on a Tarot card has its own meaning. As a child, I was always terrible at mathematics. Somehow, even then I had always felt

there was more to numbers than some boring mathematical equation. Numerology confirmed this intuition. I was fascinated to learn how each number had its own issues, strengths, and energies. Ones represent seeds and new beginnings. Twos are about partnership and love. Threes often show creative growth and fertility. Fours represent foundations and balance. Fives are often about conflict. Sixes show friendship and sharing. Sevens are magic and choices. Eights indicate movement. Nines show preparation. Finally, tens are completion. It quickly became apparent to me that numbers are no accident. Not only in our Tarot readings, but also in our lives, the numbers we encounter have messages for us.

Every suit in the Minor Arcana, as well as in your average playing deck, represents an element. Wands/Clubs represent Fire, Pentacles/Diamonds represent Earth, Swords/Spades represent Air, and Cups/Hearts represent Water. These elements are repeated in the zodiac, and its symbols often appear in these cards. As the Major Arcana refers to astrological signs, my next subject of interest naturally became astrology.

I fell in love with astrology almost immediately. Originally, it was just fun to research my own sign. I spent time reading descriptions of Aries' traits in various books to see what was me, and what wasn't. After that I started looking up the astrological signs of close friends and family. For the most part, I found the astrological portraits to be accurate enough, and I became interested in knowing other people's sun signs.

When I asked people their sun signs, I noticed how almost everyone knew and loved their own signs, and how almost everyone had strong feelings about certain other signs. Even if they weren't aware of why they felt certain ways, I heard people make statements such as, "Oh you're an Aries! I thought I liked you!" or, "Oh, I just love Pisces men."

I couldn't help but find these sociological aspects fascinating. I have always been a people-person and I was a server by trade, so the wealth of people I could draw on for information was endless.

I thought I had all the information I needed to know about every sign until I came across a book called *Linda Goodman's Love Signs* by Linda Goodman. Until this time, I had only memorized character studies of the various signs and the ways they might communicate with one another. I had no idea there was any method to this magic.

At the back of Goodman's book, she includes an index where I learned which elements rule which signs and the various jobs we share. Suddenly, instead of only memorizing the information, I was applying it to my life and the people around me. In my personal studies it became apparent to me that depending on the characteristics of our season, element, and job, we form different combinations with our fellow signs. These combinations, I learned, are made in one of seven ways. This intrigued me. Seven is my favourite number, and for me it indicates magic, intuition, and choices. I had a hunch that there was a reason there

were seven combinations. In the meantime, I compiled lists of the people I knew under their appropriate signs, and looked for links. I was looking for similarities between signs, elements, jobs, and seasons, and for commonalities in my relationships to the various signs.

This research led me to see astrology through a whole new perspective. Instead of telling a person what their traits were after they told me their signs, I was telling people about their astrological jobs, their elements, and our mutual combination with one another.

While browsing in one of my favourite mystic bookstores, I happened upon a chakra system chart. I had never heard of chakras before. Noticing that there were seven chakras, I immediately bought the chart. I wondered if these seven chakras might have any connection to our seven sun-sign combinations. In 2001, I made a list of the seven sun sign combinations, and matched them up with the seven chakras in a journal entry. I assumed this information was out there already, but I just hadn't found it yet. Time passed, and while I read many more books on astrology, none addressed this connection.

Nine years later, I serendipitously stumbled upon my next clue. Thanks to two spiritual-healing teachers, what started as an aura scan quickly evolved into my first course on energy. I followed this with Reiki 1 and Reiki 2. Through these courses I learned again about the seven chakras and their corresponding energies. The more I learned and studied about these energy

points, the more familiar they sounded. In 2010 I found
a connection between astrology and the chakras. The
result is this book. Please enjoy with Love.

Part 1. How to Use this Book

This book works with your Spirit, which I will also call your energy or subtle body. Whenever we do Spirit work we are tapping into the unseen energy of the universe. We can see our bodies, and so we often think this is all that we are. We think of Spirit at death, but live our lives in our personalities or Egos, often ignoring Spirit at work in and around us.

How Does your Spirit Speak to You?

It is most important that you recognize your own Spirit and learn how to separate your Spirit's voice from your Ego when needed. For the longest time, I had recurring dreams of being in a car and having no control of the brakes or steering wheel. It took me years to figure out that I was the vehicle out of control and my Spirit was the concerned driver behind the wheel.

In cartoons, Ego and Spirit are often portrayed as the devil and the angel. While the Ego is not necessarily a devil since it is necessary for physical survival, its only concern is you, you, you. Our Spirit, on the other hand, has everyone's best interest at heart. As spiritual beings, we come to human form to do more than survive, or even survive well. We come with a divine purpose.

Since Spirit is our connection to the Divine, Spirit will always give our Ego free will, even if it has a master plan. There are various subtle ways our energy communicates this divine will to us. No matter what mistakes we may be making, our Spirit will never abandon us, and it loves to leave the clues we need to learn. These messages are encoded in our lives, much like they are in Tarot.

What numbers follow us? What colours are we drawn to? What scents appeal to us? What music do we love? In what season were we born? What element rules us? What animals do we connect with? What gemstones are we intrigued by? What is our job? What astrological signs are we naturally drawn to or repelled by? These are all hints as to what Spirit really has planned for us, and what we need to survive.

Spirit gives us a natural instinct to self-heal. We are unconsciously drawn to what we need. When I studied Reiki, I learned about healing through touch. It is interesting to me that when we hurt ourselves, the first thing we instinctively do is grab that part of our bodies. And who doesn't kiss their child's boo-boo? I believe Spirit provides a natural healing instinct in us all.

While our energy cannot force us, it can passively guide us toward survival. For example, you may choose to drink beer every night. That is Ego's choice. However, the colour of your beer label may just be Spirit's choice. It is a subtle way our energy not only communicates with us, but also tries to heal the same parts we may be harming. Most of us have a favourite fast food joint. Our feel-good food may have more to do with the colours of the restaurant's logo than the nutrients of the food. Colour is one way our Spirit heals us. We wear clothing, buy cars, and paint our houses with colour, and yet so few of us realize why we choose to involve these colours in our lives. Yet behind our choices, every colour is connected to a chakra, and our chosen colours often scream of significance when we start to relate the two.

For example, while volunteering at a seniors' home, I became aware of how many people wore purple, and how often. Purple is the colour of the crown chakra, which is our connection to the Divine. One of my friends at the home uses a walker to get around. One day, when we were talking about colour, she said, "I never leave the house without some red on. What does that mean?" I chuckled. Red is the colour of the root chakra, which grounds us to the earth. When we are rooted, we cannot fall. So you see, Spirit counsels. Spirit leaves a path, because it truly wants to be revealed and enjoyed in each of us.

Sun Sign Astrology and Chakra Sun Signs as Tools for Spiritual Introspection

In the same way Spirit draws us to the colours we need, it draws us to the sun signs we need. I believe our astrological friends have an energy much like colour to offer us. In times of need, we are drawn to the sun signs, and hence, to the energy we require.

Chakra Sun Signs is meant to be used as a tool for spiritual introspection. This book is about the role we play in the universe, as well as the vital information others have to give us. We have so many jobs to do here on this earth. While some may be our actual careers, others are universal responsibilities.

Most of us already know our own sun signs. For the purpose of this book, it is just as important to know the signs of those around you. How far you choose to go with this is up to you. You could ask close friends and family, branch out to co-workers, or even get so curious as to ask that annoying client, or your child's teacher. I have even been bold enough to ask prospective employers.

Some people are more open to astrology than others, so depending on who you are asking, a simple "When's your birthday?" will suffice. It is not really important that they know why you are asking as you are not taking this information to learn about them as much as you are seeking knowledge about yourself. For example, if you recently started a new job and really clicked with everyone except one person, you could simply ask the person, "When's your Birthday?" This may just break the ice all on its own. In any event, you could take the information and use what I provide in this book to figure out what you have in common with this person, or what the two of you may have to teach each other.

In my own experiences, once I understand what I have in common with a person, or what we have to teach each other, my relationship with that person usually changes for the better. When I meet people, I often tell them the colour and the chakra in which we connect. More often than not, I get a positive response, and sometimes even a light-bulb moment. It has often been said that the world we see is a reflection of ourselves. The characteristics we don't like in others usually mirror the parts of ourselves that we don't like. The same is true of the characteristics we like in others. This book is designed to help you understand exactly what parts of yourself you are looking at when you connect with other people.

For this reason, it is necessary that you learn all the signs, and the job, season and element of each, as well as your own Chakra Sun Signs. Don't be scared; I will share all this information in the following chapters. Your job is to apply it. It is also vital that you understand the seven chakras. I provide enough information to get you started, but it is your own studies that will astound you. You can always reference the books from my selected bibliography, but never underestimate the power of your own Spirit to find the books that speak to you.

I am a huge fan of keeping it simple, and so I break down the thought process behind this theory in a way that is both accessible and relevant. It is my hope that this information will be as natural to grasp for newcomers as it is for those already familiar with astrology or the chakra system. When you read the chapters ahead, you will notice I have included some charts for you to complete. Please take the time to do this, as these charts should help you learn to identify the elements, jobs, and energy available to you from each sun sign in your life. You should also notice patterns between your different relationships and the chakras they align with. For years and years, sun signs have been considered by many as entertainment, or at best a definition of Ego and not Spirit. Sun sign and chakra combinations is a new theory. I look forward to hearing what you will learn about yourself.

Once you become familiar with these combinations, you will likely realize that this energy has always been present in your life. When I began to recall situations from my past that had revolved around certain chakras, I noticed that the people I needed had always been there. Even if my Ego didn't know why I was where I was, or with whom, my Spirit always knew. I have included some personal stories of these types of situations in the case studies section. I think it is important to note that I was unaware of my own Chakra Sun Signs when most of these experiences took place.

Part 2. What is a Chakra?

A Description of the Chakra System and the Associated Modes of Healing

Everything is energy. Science has proven that even the most solid substances are actually comprised of millions of tiny particles of energy whirling around. Human beings are no different. We are energy constantly interacting with other energies. One of the ways we absorb the energy we need is through our chakras. The word chakra comes from the language of Sanskrit and translates to wheel of light or vortex. Knowledge of these wheels has long been taught in Ayurvedic medicine and dates back to the time before the first recording of Christ.

While our bodies are made up of hundreds of minor chakras, there are seven main wheels of light known as the chakra system. These all have a location in the subtle body as well as in the physical body. Much like the gears of a clock, the chakras start at the base of the spine and rotate in clockwise and counter clockwise directions upward to the crown of the head. Along with being a source of energy for each other, the wheels generate the subtle body and coincide with the endocrine glands, the nerve plexus, the organs, and other parts of the physical body. Each chakra also has specific emotional issues, identities, and lessons to learn. The idea is that when all chakra levels are balanced and operating equally, we can attain spiritual enlightenment and perfect health.

Chakras one through three represent our physical self and our connection to the world. Chakras five through seven relate to our spiritual self and our connection to the Divine. The fourth chakra, the heart, rests in the middle and is the communicator for these two polarities. Ideally we want to live in balance.

Your chakras may be balanced and healthy, underactive, overactive, blocked, or a mixture of all of these.

People seeking a healthy and balanced chakra system may use a variety of healing methods.

Each wheel vibrates to its own colour and tone, so hues and harmony are often used for healing. Gemstones can be placed on chakra centres, or carried to heal or charge energy. Many paths of yoga include postures to awaken the light in each of these wheels. Chakras also respond to aromatherapy, Reiki, meditation, mantras, affirmations, and the colourful nutrients of fruits and vegetables. On the following pages you will find beautiful illustrations for meditation on the seven chakras and a brief summary of each, including the location, body parts, colours, and issues associated with each wheel and suggested applications for healing.

Root Chakra

LOCATION:	Base of spine/coccyx
BODY PARTS:	Legs and feet (including hips, knees, ankles, and toes); colon; and all bones

The Root chakra deals with all physical realms of our lives. This is the source of the body's endurance and our connection to the earth. This is the tribal chakra which relates to both our own family as well as to the non-familial tribes we form throughout our lives. Fear is triggered here. The main issue of our Root chakra is survival.

COLOURS:	Red and Brown
YOGA POSTURES:	Child's Pose, The Thunderbolt
MANTRAS:	Lam/Sring
AFFIRMATION:	I trust the process of life.
GEMSTONES:	Red Jasper, Ruby, Fortified Wood
AROMAS:	Cinnamon, Cedar
SOUND:	Do
FOODS:	Raspberries, Tomatoes, Red Peppers, Cherries, Radishes

Sacral Chakra

LOCATION:	Lower abdomen
BODY PARTS:	Pelvic area, lower back, kidneys, reproductive organs, and adrenal glands

The Sacral chakra deals with issues of desire, choice, and manifestation of movement. This chakra is largely responsible for our relationships, finances, and sexuality. It is also a vital source of our creativity. The Sacral chakra is where all life energy is stored. The main issue of our Sacral chakra is choice of movement or flow.

COLOUR:	Orange
YOGA POSTURES:	The Locust, The Cobra
MANTRAS:	Vam/Hring
AFFIRMATION:	I freely create my choices.
GEMSTONES:	Orange Calcite, Carnelian
AROMAS:	Ylang Ylang, Orange Blossom, Juniper
SOUND:	Re
FOODS:	Carrots, Sweet Potatoes, Tangerines, Pumpkins

Solar Plexus Chakra

Solar plexus

Digestive system, stomach, liver, pancreas, gallbladder, small and large intestines, spleen, and middle spine

The Solar Plexus chakra deals with empowerment, Ego, and self-esteem. This chakra works with our personality and the way we choose to express ourselves to the world. It is largely responsible for our personal identity and activities. The main issue of the Solar Plexus chakra is personal power.

Yellow

The Bridge, Crescent Boat

Ram/Kling

I trust my inner fire.

Citrine, Tiger's Eye

Lemon, Grapefruit

Me

Pineapples, Corn, Yellow Beans, Bananas

Heart Chakra

LOCATION: Chest

BODY PARTS: Heart, lungs, breasts, upper back, shoulders, arms, and hands

The Heart chakra deals with lessons of love, emotions, and equilibrium. The Heart chakra is the communicator for the whole chakra system and responsible for how our chakras function as a team. It is where we learn about compassion for others, as well as ourselves. It is here that we learn about the balance of all things. The main issue of the Heart chakra is unconditional love.

COLOURS: Green and Pink

YOGA POSTURES: Head of Cow, The Triangle

MANTRAS: Yam/Bhring

AFFIRMATION: Love is in and around me always.

GEMSTONES: Jade, Emerald, Rose Quartz

AROMAS: Pine, Eucalyptus

SOUND: Fa

FOODS: Pink Grapefruit, Spinach, Broccoli, Kiwi

Throat Chakra

Base of throat

Throat; neck; ears; sinuses; the mouth including teeth, gums, and jaw; thyroid; and parathyroid

The Throat chakra deals with our communication. It governs how well we listen and how clearly we speak. This chakra controls our voice, which in turn creates our world. The way we express ourselves directly affects the lives we lead. For this reason, the Throat chakra is also considered a chakra of creativity. The main issue of the Throat chakra is being aware of your word, or speaking the truth.

Blue

The Fish, Lion's Pose

Ham/Lring

Positive words create my world.

Lapis lazuli, Blue tourmaline

Peppermint, Basil

So

Blueberries, Blue Potatoes, Blue Grapes

Third Eye Chakra

LOCATION: Base of forehead

BODY PARTS: Lower brain, nervous system, and pituitary gland

The Third Eye chakra deals with realms of consciousness, perception, and memory. This chakra is the centre of our intuition and psychic abilities. It is responsible for our dreams, imaginations, and the ability to recognize synchronicity in our lives. The main issue of the Third Eye chakra is inner wisdom.

COLOUR: Indigo

YOGA POSTURES: Chanting Om, Eye Exercises

MANTRAS: Om/Soham

AFFIRMATION: I freely follow my intuition.

GEMSTONES: Azurite, Sodalite

AROMAS: Rosemary, Lime

SOUND: La

FOODS: Blackberries, Blueberries, Eggplant

Crown Chakra

LOCATION:	Crown of head
BODY PART:	Pineal gland

The Crown chakra deals with all areas of Spirit. This chakra is our connection to the Divine. Universal energy enters here, making it possible for experiences of peace and fulfilment. Issues of faith and belief systems are formed here. The main issue of the Crown chakra is enlightenment.

COLOUR:	Purple
YOGA POSTURES:	Shoulder Stand, The Hare
MANTRAS:	Purnam/Silence
AFFIRMATION:	I am my world.
GEMSTONES:	Amethyst, Quartz (clear)
AROMAS:	Lavender, Patchouli, Frankincense
SOUND:	Te
FOODS:	Grapes, Cauliflower, Purple or White Onions, Coconuts

The Zodiac Wheel

Many of us love to wear clothes and eat foods that are beautifully coloured. We are drawn to certain music, or we carry gemstones. Perhaps we practice aromatherapy, affirmations, or yoga. Whether we are aware of our own chakra system or not, it is my belief that our Spirit subconsciously guides us to these healing methods. I can attest that long before I was aware of my chakras, I was drawn to their specific colours. I remember coming home from the convenience store and noticing with amusement that I had bought all orange-packaged items. That was well before I knew about the energy of colour. On the same note, I have always collected gemstones. It wasn't until I met my energy teachers in Nova Scotia that I understood why. Along with these treatments, I believe there is one more element that interfaces with the chakras: our fellow sun signs. Not all of us practice yoga or carry gemstones, but we are all interacting with our fellow signs of the zodiac.

Part 3. Sun Signs

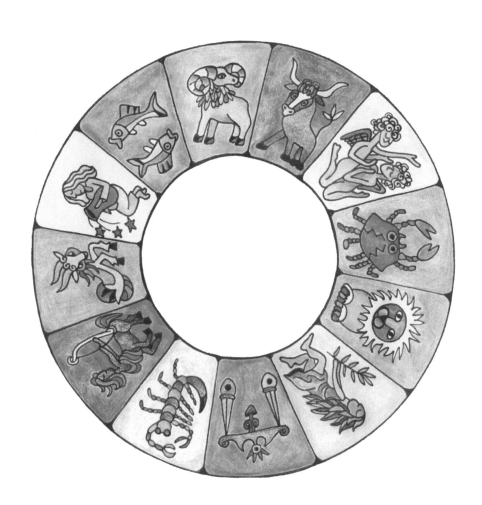

Definition of Sun Signs

Your sun sign is determined by the zodiac sign that the sun was in on the day you were born. The following chart contains the signs and the birth dates of each sign in the zodiac wheel. In the spaces provided in Figure 1, write down the names of the people you know next to their appropriate signs. If the birth date of the person you know falls on the first or last day of their sun sign, then a little more research may be involved. In addition to their date of birth, for these folks you will need to know their time of birth and the internet to tell you what sign the sun was in at that particular point in the day.

Figure 1. Friends and Family Sun Sign Date Chart

Sun Sign	Dates	People You Know
Aries	March 20 – April 20	
Taurus	April 20 – May 21	
Gemini	May 21 – June 21	
Cancer	June 21 – July 22	

Leo	July 22 – August 23	
Virgo	August 23 – September 23	
Libra	September 23 – October 23	
Scorpio	October 23 – November 22	
Sagittarius	November 22 – December 21	
Capricorn	December 21 – January 20	
Aquarius	January 20 – February 19	
Pisces	February 19 – March 20	

Part 4. Why Sun Signs?

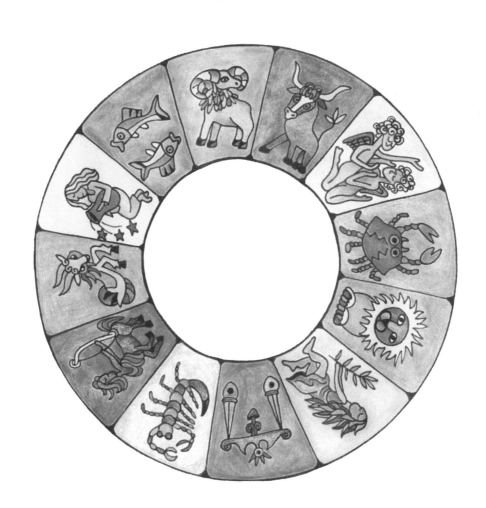

While few of us possess the skill to cast an astrological chart, almost all of us know what our own sun sign is. Some of us read about our sun sign in the newspaper every day. This is the sign you may have tattooed on your body. While this is by no means our whole astrological story, our sun sign is, arguably, the most recognizable influence in our charts. Not only can we see ourselves in our sign, others can see our sign in us.

I don't believe this is an accident. Each person born under a particular sun sign has a job to do. It is important that we be recognizable to others when needed. It is also imperative that we understand who we are and the universal role our Spirits designed for us on the day we were born.

Part 5. Elements, Jobs, and Seasons

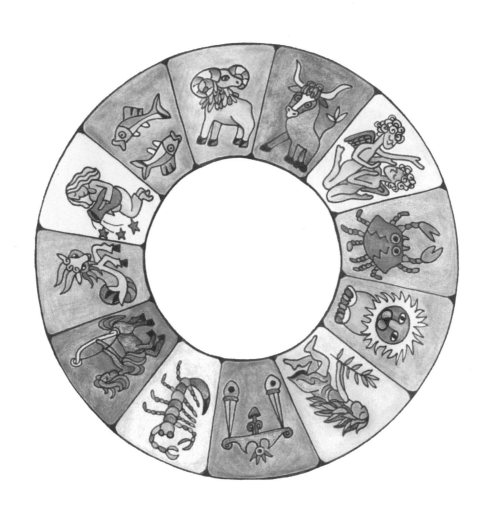

The Elements: Fire, Earth, Air, and Water

The zodiac is made up of twelve signs. Within these twelve signs there are four repeating elements: FIRE, EARTH, AIR, and WATER. Each sun sign expresses the characteristics of its particular element. These characteristics tend to mirror the element itself. For example, Fire signs tend to be fiery and charismatic. Earth signs tend to be secure and stubborn. Air signs tend to be expressive and idealistic. Finally, Water signs tend to be immense and receptive. Therefore, depending on the element we are working for, our areas of speciality vary. Fire rules inspiration and creativity. Earth rules foundations and stability. Air rules intellect and communication. Water rules emotions, love, and friendship.

Just like in Mother Nature, each element has natural characteristics that affect how this element blends with other elements. For example, Fire and Air can blend easily, but require effort to work with Earth and Fire. Earth and Water can blend easy, but require effort to work with Fire and Air. Regardless of the combination, no one element is stronger than any other, and we all have the same ability to influence or to endure one another. For example, although Fire and Air can blend, Fire can suffocate Air and Air can extinguish Fire. Earth and Water can blend, but Earth can devour Water and Water can destroy Earth. Even amongst the same element there are dangers. Too much of the same element can result in a storm.

The Jobs: Leaders, Organizers, and Communicators

As astrological signs, we work for our element. Each element of the zodiac and season of the year is appointed its own leader, organizer, and communicator. These responsibilities are incorporated into our signs.

Now, if you have a job to do for the universe, don't you want to know what it is? The job titles are listed in Figure 2.

Figure 2. Sun Sign Elements, Jobs, and Seasons

Job Title	Sun Sign	Season
Fire Leader	Aries	Spring
Fire Organizer	Leo	Summer
Fire Communicator	Sagittarius	Fall
Water Leader	Cancer	Summer
Water Organizer	Scorpio	Fall
Water Communicator	Pisces	Winter
Air Leader	Libra	Fall
Air Organizer	Aquarius	Winter
Air Communicator	Gemini	Spring
Earth Leader	Capricorn	Winter
Earth Organizer	Taurus	Spring
Earth Communicator	Virgo	Summer

Our personalities vary depending on our jobs. Leaders are born at the beginning of each season and are cardinal in nature, which means they thrive on change and have an impulsive energy. Organizers are born in the middle of each season, and are fixed in nature, which means they are not comfortable with change and have a more resolute energy. Communicators are born at the end of each season and are mutable in nature, which means they are practical with change and have a more adaptable energy.

The Seasons

The season we are born in also has its significance. People born in the spring are the children of the zodiac, meaning they do their jobs in an instinctive way. People born in the summer are the adolescents of the zodiac, meaning they do their jobs in an ingenious way. People born in the fall are the adults of the zodiac, meaning they do their jobs in an influential way. People born in the winter are the seniors of the zodiac, meaning they do their jobs in an insightful way.

The elements, jobs, and seasons create different relationships amongst the signs. By referencing the personal friends and family list you created in Figure 1, you can find comparisons between your sign and those of your loved ones based on the seasons, jobs, and elements represented by your sun sign. Perhaps you share the same element as your favourite cousin, and never realized it. Or, think about the uncle who always picks on you for the way you do things. He may have the same job as you, be it Leader, Organizer, or Communicator, but he may also have a non-blending element of either Fire, Earth, Air, or Water. Once you have this information, it is much easier to understand the various roles played in the zodiac, and to respect everyone's purpose.

If you are struggling with a particular problem, or require assistance, understanding the sun signs can help you know who to call for help. We have much to learn from every sign, and we would be wise to familiarize ourselves with each one. The beauty of this is that we are all equally important as the elements we represent. Whether a servant or a Prime Minister, each of us has a purpose greater than our actual careers.

In fact, one of the most common questions I am asked about sun sign astrology is "What signs are bad for me?" Personally, I think we need to meet with all twelve job titles in the zodiac since we each have our own areas of expertise. Maybe that's why there were twelve Disciples at the Last Supper.

Part 6. The Seven Sun Sign Combinations

Seven Sun Sign Combinations

While there is no doubting the significance of the twelve zodiac signs in our lives, little light has been shed on the seven different ways we meet one another.

Depending on our elements, jobs, and placements on the wheel, we combine with our fellow sun signs in one of seven ways.

How to Use the Seven Sun Sign Combinations Chart

In Figure 3, you will find the 12 zodiac signs listed in order. Locate your own zodiac sign on the chart, and write the number 1 in the space provided. Now, moving down the page, continue to number the signs after your own in sequence until you reach number 7. If you come to the bottom of the column before you reach number 7, continue your counting at the top of the column working your way back down until you reach the number.

Next, return to your own sign and repeat the same number sequence in the opposite direction. If you come to the top of the column and are not at number 7, continue your counting at the bottom of the column and work your way back up until you reach the number.

For example, if you are a Leo, your chart will look like Figure 4 below. It doesn't matter where your sign may fall in the zodiac. For this exercise, count your own zodiac sign as number 1.

When you finish there should be a number no higher than 7 beside every sign. You should have one number 1 and one number 7, two number 2s, two number 3s, two number 4s, two number 5s, and two number 6s. These numbers are the guide to your seven sun sign combinations.

Figure 3. Seven Sun Sign Combinations Chart

Aries	
Taurus	
Gemini	
Cancer	
Leo	
Virgo	
Libra	
Scorpio	
Sagittarius	
Capricorn	
Aquarius	
Pisces	

Figure 4. Completed Example of a Leo's Combinations Chart

Aries	5
Taurus	4
Gemini	3
Cancer	2
Leo	1
Virgo	2
Libra	3
Scorpio	4
Sagittarius	5
Capricorn	6
Aquarius	7
Pisces	6

Description of the Seven Sun Sign Combinations

Combination # 1 connects you with the people who share your sun sign. This means that they have the same job, element, season, and placement on the wheel as you. The fact that you have so much in common means you tend to like the people in your life who have these signs, and you tend to know them very well. These are usually very long, loyal relationships in your life.

Combination # 2 connects you with your seasonal/karmic neighbours. These are the people who sit in the houses on either side of your own in the zodiac, representing the time of season directly before your sign and the time of season directly after your sign. They do not share your job, nor do they have elements that match or blend effortlessly with your own. Due to these reasons, you can have powerful reactions to these signs. If you don't love them, you often tolerate them.

Combination # 3 connects you with the people whose element blends favourably with your own. They have different jobs than you, but the harmonious nature of this combination means that you are usually in the same field of study. These are your feel-good friends. The fact that your elements complement one another means that your interests, ideas, and creativity are often inspired around these folks.

Combination # 4 connects you with the people who have the same job as you, but with elements that do not match or blend effortlessly with your own. Since these folks do the same job as you but in different ways, there is often an awkward introduction to this relationship. There is a tendency to feel either inferior or superior around these signs. Once equality is established, however, you can become powerful allies.

Combination # 5 connects you with the people that share your element, and hold the other two jobs besides your own job that work for your element (Leader, Organizer, or Communicator). The fact that you share

elements with these people means you often have an ease of communication around them. Your different jobs mean you have valuable information to learn and share regarding your element.

Combination # 6 connects you with the people that appear to have nothing in common with your sun sign. Unlike all your other combinations, you are far in placement from these signs, hold different seasons and jobs, and have elements that neither match nor blend effortlessly. Due to these reasons, we run into these signs less often than the others, and we are usually brought together in roundabout ways. It is not uncommon to be intrigued by this combination as their differences make them very interesting to us.

Combination # 7 connects you with the people who share your job and have the element that blends effortlessly with your own. This sign sits on the opposite side of the wheel from you. Because of this, your lives often complement or include each other in equal yet opposite ways. Very often you will find this combination close by, as these folks are at the same place as you, but for a different and yet symbiotic reason.

Part 7. How To Find Your Chakra Sun Signs

The same chart and numbers you used to find your seven sun sign combinations also unlock the door to your Chakra Sun Signs. The number beside each sun sign also symbolizes the specific chakra in which you meet up with those signs.

In Figure 5 you will find the seven numbered chakras. Next to each number, write down the sign or signs that fall beside them in your combinations chart.

Figure 5. Chakra Sun Signs Chart

The Chakras	Your Chakra Sun Signs
# 1. Root Chakra (Red)	# 1.
# 2. Sacral Chakra (Orange)	# 2.
# 3. Solar Plexus Chakra (Yellow)	# 3.
# 4. Heart Chakra (Green)	# 4.
# 5. Throat Chakra (Blue)	# 5.
# 6. Third Eye Chakra (Indigo)	# 6.
# 7. Crown Chakra (Purple)	# 7.

Continuing with the Leo example, Figure 6 shows a Leo's Chakra Sun Sign chart.

Figure 6. Chakra Sun Signs Chart for a Leo

Chakras	Your Chakra Sun Signs
# 1. Root Chakra (Red)	# 1. Leo
# 2. Sacral Chakra (Orange)	# 2. Cancer and Virgo
# 3. Solar Plexus Chakra (Yellow)	# 3. Gemini and Libra
# 4. Heart Chakra (Green)	# 4. Taurus and Scorpio
# 5. Throat Chakra (Blue)	# 5. Aries and Sagittarius
# 6. Third Eye Chakra (Indigo)	# 6. Capricorn and Pisces
# 7. Crown Chakra (Purple)	# 7. Aquarius

The Seven Unique Chakra Sun Sign Friendships

After you have completed your chart, you may start to notice connections between the different chakras and the sun sign combinations they align with. No matter what job your sun sign has, you meet up with the other sun signs who share that job in your Root, Heart, and Crown chakras. I believe these meetings occur to triple affirm and support what our Spirits came to earth to do for the Divine. The coincidences don't stop there.

Our first chakra, the Root, is our connection to the earth. It holds our tribal energy. How appropriate that we should meet the people who share our sign in this energy centre. After all, they came to the earth in the same season as we did to do the same job with the same element.

Our second chakra, the Sacral, is all about choices. How fitting that we should meet our astrological neighbours here. Representing where we have come from and where we are going, they help us to make the right choices for our present.

Our third chakra, the Solar Plexus, is our personal power centre, ruling our self esteem. We meet up here with the people whose element complements our own. These folks make us feel good, and we can mutually benefit from our blending element.

Our fourth chakra, the Heart, is in charge of unconditional love and equilibrium. Interestingly enough, we meet up here with the people who do the same job we do, but who have elements that do not blend effortlessly with our own. This match is clearly a challenge that must involve love and balance.

Our fifth chakra, the Throat, is responsible for voice, communication, and speaking our truth. Magically, we meet up here with the people who hold different jobs, but who are under the same element as we are. It is therefore easy to talk to and listen to these signs. Not only do they have information to give us, but they also speak our language.

Our sixth chakra, the Third Eye, rules the unconscious and psychic realm. This energy centre stores the hidden and often untapped part of ourselves. Fancy that we should meet here the only signs in the zodiac that do not share proximity, season, element, or job with us. This relationship is not an obvious connection, and it takes time or synchronicity to form.

Our seventh chakra, the Crown, is our connection to the universal energy. Profoundly, we meet up with our equal opposite here. This sign sits exactly across the wheel from us, it is the furthest away from us, and yet it shares our job and complements our element. With these folks we can see the whole spectrum of the wheel differently but at the same level.

These connections are more than just a fluke. These numbers match for a reason. We all have energy for one another, we all have messages to give, and we all have Chakra Sun Signs.

Part 8. What are Chakra Sun Signs?

Chakra Sun Signs

Researchers and lovers of spirituality have attempted to combine the chakra system and zodiac before. Yet until now, no one has noticed this simple truth. Sun sign astrology is not meant to be a complicated mathematical equation, nor is it simply a description of our Egos. Sun sign astrology is actually the study of the universal consciousness and the small parts we all play in this consciousness. Every one of us has a team of sun sign consultants looking out for us and generating energy for our various chakras. As spiritual beings, we are all sources of light for one another.

The sun's light can be divided inside a prism into the seven colours of the rainbow. As members of the zodiac, we are all prisms holding healing colours! Imagine the zodiac's wheel as a massive flat circle of snow. If you looked more closely, you'd realize you were actually looking at billions of individual snowflakes collected in one spot. We are all white light; however, the sun hits different snowflakes at different angles, so depending on where you look, you can see every colour of the rainbow. Furthermore, the colour by which you view another snowflake is the same colour by which that snowflake views you. When we interact with other signs we make different colours and create changes in our energy.

Our Chakra Sun Signs are in our lives to teach, aid, challenge, or communicate with us about specific areas of energy. These relationships can be mutually beneficial, accommodating, or challenging, and they are formed in any number of ways. People are drawn to and repelled by others all the time. I think that all exchanges of energy happen for a reason. In the following sections you will find the Chakra Sun Signs for every sign in the zodiac as well as my own personal case studies on each of these seven important friendships. These are meant to provide you with examples of how the various relationships in our lives intertwine with our seven chakras.

Part 9. Root Chakra Friendship

Root Chakra Friends at a Glance

Aries-Aries	Libra-Libra
Taurus-Taurus	Scorpio-Scorpio
Gemini-Gemini	Sagittarius-Sagittarius
Cancer-Cancer	Capricorn-Capricorn
Leo-Leo	Aquarius-Aquarius
Virgo-Virgo	Pisces-Pisces

What your Root chakra friends might say…

It is safe here . . . Is it safe here?

The Root chakra rests at the base of the spine. This is our connection to the earth. As we have only one earth, it makes sense that there is only one sun sign that connects with this chakra. Our Root friends share our sign in the zodiac. These are the people who have the same job, season, house, and element as we do in this lifetime. Root friends are in our lives to remind us of who we are and why we came to the earth in the season we did. Our Root friends can often generate the tribal power within us, which means we usually admire and feel at home with these folks. This may sound biased, but we generally love them and understand their faults because they remind us of ourselves.

Case Study of Root Chakra Friendship

Our mutual connection to the earth means we often have very long, solid relationships with these people, or feel safe in their company. As a baby, I was adopted by a family with a Root mama, a Root brother, and Root grandma. Growing up I always knew I wanted to have a child one day, mainly because I wanted to know what it was like to live with someone who was like me. Now a mother, I find it poetic that my only son and me also meet in the Root chakra. Not only is he my blood, he also shares my tribe. Three of my oldest friends are also Root connections.

The Root chakra is the source of our physical well-being. It rules the colon, which works at eliminating the bad things from our system. Our Root chakra friends often aid us in this way, encouraging us toward good and away from harm.

One of my oldest Root friends is a dentist. A year ago, when I was financially strapped, she called me to make an appointment to have my teeth checked. I had no money, and I hate going to the dentist, but my friend insisted on a free check up. When I went, she found a wisdom tooth that needed removal. Once again, I resisted. It wasn't giving me any trouble and I couldn't afford it! My friend would not take no for

an answer. She made me another appointment and she extracted the tooth free of charge. When I saw the tooth, I almost died! It was black. The whole procedure was relatively painless because I felt safe. I would never have had that tooth removed if it wasn't for my Root friend, at least not before it became an unbearable problem.

The Root chakra also encompasses the feet and legs that we use to move away from harm and toward help. In fact, our fight or flight tendencies are formed here. My oldest Root friend and I met on the swings in grade two. He was new to the school, and I was an outcast. Together we quickly became friends and planned our escape from the schoolyard at lunch the following day.

At 12:35 the next day we made our break. We waited until the duty teacher went around the corner of the school as we suspiciously picked flowers by the exit gate. As soon as the teacher was out of sight we started to sprint. As we crossed from the schoolyard threshold to the open world, schoolmates began to scream. We didn't care. We were going to live off apples and Halloween candy, and make a fort in the woods. We would have done it too, had my friend not slipped and cut his knee. I remember this like it was yesterday. We were two dramatic seven-year-olds arguing; he wanted to continue, and I wanted to get a bandage for his bloody knee. All of this went on with a duty teacher hot on the scent of tattle tales. While our great escape fell through that day, we have remained best friends all these years, and we are both still flighters, not fighters.

If your Root friends aren't helping you to feel secure and healthy, you may need to ask yourself why. Is it safe where you are? Challenges with your own sign can be an indication that your own life may be unstable in some way. Our similarities can sometimes bring out the bad as well as the good qualities in each other. For instance, it is not uncommon to have the mentality of invincibility around these signs. When this happens, we should remember that our Root friends are not here to validate our bad habits, but rather to mirror our own shortcomings so that we might see them in ourselves.

It is also unwise to fight with these friends, as inevitably you will both feel insecure. I have often witnessed this sort of challenge in work or friend/family dynamics when there is only one position but two equal players vying for the same title or decision. I have had my share of bouts with many of the Root friends in my life. We have so much in common with these folks that when we aren't loving them, we just may be loathing them. They are tough to beat as they have all the same tricks up their sleeves as we do. Trust me when

I say it is always better to work with this sign, so that you may be each other's biggest fans.

Part 10. Sacral Chakra Friendship

Sacral Chakra Friends at a Glance

Aries-Taurus & Pisces	Libra-Virgo & Scorpio
Taurus-Aries & Gemini	Scorpio-Libra & Sagittarius
Gemini-Taurus & Cancer	Sagittarius-Scorpio & Capricorn
Cancer-Gemini & Leo	Capricorn-Sagittarius & Aquarius
Leo-Cancer & Virgo	Aquarius-Capricorn & Pisces
Virgo-Leo & Libra	Pisces-Aquarius & Aries

What your Sacral chakra friends might say…

There is always a choice . . . There is no choice.

Since the Sacral chakra rules what choices we make, it seems only necessary that our Sacral chakra friends provide us with options. These folks are our next-door neighbours in astrology, meaning they were born in either the sign right before our own or in the sun sign directly after our own. Our Sacral chakra friends have different jobs and elements that do not match or blend easily with our own, and yet they are the signs that rest in the houses on either side of us. Sound like your neighbourhood? Due to these reasons, we can have powerful reactions to this combination.

The closeness of our houses means we are also karmically close in soul age with these signs. They have the proximity to look into our house and often they have options or advice to give from across the fence. This can sometimes seem too close for comfort, and depending on what our Sacral friends are saying, we can feel an intense like or dislike for this association.

Case Study of Sacral Chakra Friendship

The sign directly ahead of our own is more likely to intimidate us as these people represent lessons we have yet to learn. We are often more endearing to the sign directly behind us as they represent lessons already learned. When you were in grade seven, who intimidated you more, the grade eights or the grade sixes? In my childhood, I can remember being intimidated by more than one Taurus. As an adult, it is more often that I esteem them for some quality I have yet to possess. On the other hand, I have had many soft spots for Pisces, and generally feel at ease in their company. Perhaps it is just part of my human condition to look back rather than forward.

I am pained by looking back at a time of my life when I was in my mid-twenties. I had decided to move to a strange big city all alone, and rent a room from an acquaintance of a friend. First I went on a cross-country tour and visited friends and family along the way. When I finally arrived at my new rented room in my new city I was broke, jobless, and pregnant. I had enough money to pay the month's rent, and maybe three hundred dollars in cash. I was not in a relationship or near the father, and I was very far away from home. From these circumstances I faced the hardest decision I have ever had to make. I spoke to the father of my unborn child, and devastated and scared, we made the choice to have an abortion.

My plan was to go through the whole thing alone. I wasn't close enough to my roommate to ask for support. In my shame, I also felt I didn't deserve any. Two nights before the scheduled abortion, a Sacral chakra friend who was living several hours away called out of the orange. When I confessed what I was planning, my friend was uncompromising. He insisted on hanging up the phone to call his work and make appropriate arrangements to be with me.

Since these friends have different perspectives, they can show us new things, or help us in ways our own element could not. If our element is out of control for instance, our Sacral chakra friends can provide great solace. In this case, I did not have the ability to ask for help. However, my Sacral neighbour looked out his window and noticed my Aries house was on Fire. He used the Water from his Pisces house to save me.

Eight months later, I was living in Jasper when an old roommate passed through town. She had been living in the Yukon, and was now on her way back home, driving solo in her own camper van cross country. We went camping together during the visit, and she showed me how she had learned to sing and play the guitar. I also learned she was pregnant, and keeping her baby. Not a man in sight. She is my other next-door neighbour, a Taurus who came to organize my foundations and stability.

Wealth and finances are also a big part of this chakra. Therefore, our orange friends can often guide our choices in this area as well. The only raise I ever received as a waitress was from a Sacral chakra boss. I had been offered another job, and while it was further away, the job was promising more hours and better shifts. When I told my boss I was leaving, she asked what she could offer me to stay. Thanks to her, I stopped to look at all my choices. In the end, I kept my job, received a higher wage, and worked a more ideal schedule. I should also mention that this Taurus boss has a husband, three kids, a dog, owns her own business, has a home on a lake, and is at least five years younger than me. And yes I am in awe, and have a great deal of respect for her.

The challenge with this association rests in whether or not we desire our Sacral chakra friend's advice or approach to life. We are in our own houses for a reason, after all. But our Sacral friends can sometimes give the message that there is no choice. Sometimes, we have to learn our karmic lessons the hard way.

These signs can seem intimidating at times, but more often than not they are here to help guide us, support our options, remind us of where we have come from, where we want to go and, most importantly, where we are.

Part 11. Solar Plexus Friendship

Solar Plexus Chakra Friends at a Glance

Aries-Aquarius & Gemini	Libra-Leo & Sagittarius
Taurus-Pisces & Cancer	Scorpio-Virgo & Capricorn
Gemini-Aries & Leo	Sagittarius-Libra & Aquarius
Cancer-Taurus & Virgo	Capricorn-Scorpio & Pisces
Leo-Gemini & Libra	Aquarius-Sagittarius & Aries
Virgo-Cancer & Scorpio	Pisces-Capricorn & Taurus

What your Solar Plexus chakra friends might say…

You can do whatever you want to do . . . Don't do that!

The Solar Plexus chakra rules our personal power, which means it is largely responsible for how we feel about ourselves. How fitting that our Solar Plexus friends are two of the signs in the zodiac whose element blends favourably with our own. These friends give us fuel for our fire and we do the same for them: Earth and Water / Fire and Air. This means they are often the boost of confidence we need, which only makes sense, as the Solar Plexus chakra deals with our self-esteem. For this reason, we often make these friends, or are drawn to them, when we are in need of reassurance or a source of inspiration in our lives.

Case Study of Solar Plexus Friendship

My Reiki master is one of my Solar Plexus chakra friends. When we first met I was unaware of how we could benefit each other. She had a store filled with aromatherapy products, gemstones, and a private room for Reiki. I was more into occult bookstores, gemstones, and astrology. Eventually, I learned she held classes in her shop. Prompted by a co-worker, I took her course entitled "Introduction to Energy." When I listened to her speak, I couldn't believe my ears. We had so much in common spiritually, and yet we had arrived at these conclusions from completely different angles. She opened the door to energy, the chakras, and Spirit. I in turn shared my knowledge of astrology and my theory of the Chakra Sun Signs.

There is a reciprocity available between these signs and ourselves. Almost always we can benefit from each other's company. Our Solar Plexus chakra friends usually share the same passions but use different mediums to represent themselves. Aside from mama-hood, my three biggest passions are people, spirituality, and the art of the written word. Almost all of my Solar Plexus friends share at least one of these passions with me. While they may not all be writers or sun sign experts, they are painters, teachers, musicians, artists, yogis, healers, servers, poets, and parents.

My boyfriend and I are Solar Plexus chakra friends. Not only do we share a passion for our son, but he is also an artist and musician. Watching my mate write his own music and lyrics, play his guitar, or paint a beautiful picture inspires me to continue my work. These people are often our muses or mentors. Another of my dear Solar Plexus chakra friends has been my number one fan and the coach of this book through the whole writing process. It was a Solar Plexus friend who typed up the first drafts of this book for me. Another Solar Plexus friend for whom I am eternally grateful to agreed to illustrate all of the magnificent artwork in this book before I ever had a cent to give her, or a publisher to call my own. These are just a few great examples of how we can benefit from each other's elements.

The challenge with these friends is maintaining independence. As our elements often thrive together, there is always the risk of becoming dependent or possessive. Jealousy, judgement, and/or neediness may sometimes arise. If this happens, we may hear our Solar Plexus friends saying, "Don't do that!" Watch out for this, as these friends are here to promote or restore our personal power, not become the sources of it. If we concentrate on and encourage each other's individuality, we will gain confidence around these signs and feel like we can do anything.

Part 12. Heart Chakra Friendship

Heart Chakra Friends at a Glance

Aries-Cancer & Capricorn	Libra-Cancer & Capricorn
Taurus-Leo & Aquarius	Scorpio-Leo & Aquarius
Gemini-Virgo & Pisces	Sagittarius-Virgo & Pisces
Cancer-Aries & Libra	Capricorn-Aries & Libra
Leo-Taurus & Scorpio	Aquarius-Taurus & Scorpio
Virgo-Gemini & Sagittarius	Pisces-Gemini & Sagittarius

What your Heart chakra friends might say...

Follow your heart . . . Protect your heart.

Our fourth chakra is located at the heart. Unlike the other chakras, which are either upper or lower, the Heart chakra is a little more complicated as it rests in the middle and is the communicator for the whole chakra system. Similarly, our Heart friends make up one of the most delicate combinations. They are two of the signs that share the same job as us in the zodiac. These folks are here to do the same work as us, but with different, unblending elements. This can be difficult for a couple of reasons. Firstly, the fact that we do the same job in different ways can sometimes be an obstacle. We may find ourselves thinking, "I would *never* do it that way." Secondly, the Heart chakra is arguably the most guarded chakra, making it more difficult to access.

People with a blocked Heart chakra tend to live life in either the upper or lower chakras but not in a balance of both. Our Heart friends often come into our lives to encourage us to access the dimensions of ourselves we may not be comfortable with. In this way, we often see these folks as either a blessing or a curse. While there may be no apparent reason for it, it is uber easy to get uncomfortable around your Heart friends, especially while forming the friendship.

Case Study of Heart Chakra Friendship

One summer before leaving Jasper, I decided I wanted to hike the Skyline trail. This 42-kilometre trek is often said to be the nicest in the park. The mother of one of my son's friends offered to hike it with me. As she is one of my Heart friends, I immediately felt apprehensive. Sure, our sons were friends, but I wasn't sure we were the same kind of people, and it was a long hike. However, as my only other option was to walk it alone, I took my chances, and on that journey we became true friends. I am sure our Spirits were giving us both the heart-to-heart we needed, and a beautiful place and day to do it in. I am so thankful I didn't refuse. Another Heart chakra friend and former co-worker remembers me blatantly telling her, "I wasn't sure of you at first," after we'd hung out for the first time. Fifteen years later, we still talk on the phone long distance.

If we can get past the uneasy start with our Heart chakra friends, they can often show us ways to balance ourselves better, or teach us new approaches to the jobs we share. My biological parents are my two Heart chakra friends. We are three Leaders of different elements. The combination had a rough start, but over time we have learned about unconditional love. Our Heart chakra friends can be great confidants and often help us to overcome emotional issues. I always had visitations with my biological mom after the adoption. That was a deal my adopted parents made and kept. As a struggling soul, my biological mother was always very honest with me about her mistakes and the situations in her life. We can, in fact, be very candid with our Heart chakra friends and comfortable to speak our secrets. The fact that my mom and I have such an open, honest relationship really helped to heal both of our hearts.

The challenge with these signs is often fear of survival. There is the potential for one sign to dominate the relationship, thereby erasing all traces of the other's element. We can balance each other, or we can cause a flip-flop where we simply exchange one extreme for another. This risk can make us feel like we need to protect our hearts by keeping these friends at a safe distance. Once mutual respect is established, however, these folks often become our preference of who we choose to let in to the mushy world of following our hearts. They understand what it's like to do the job we do, and it is nice to have someone else around who can do it, so long as we are taking turns.

Part 13. Throat Chakra Friendship

Throat Chakra Friends at a Glance

Aries-Leo & Sagittarius	Libra-Aquarius & Gemini
Taurus-Virgo & Capricorn	Scorpio-Cancer & Pisces
Gemini-Libra & Aquarius	Sagittarius-Aries & Leo
Cancer-Scorpio & Pisces	Capricorn-Virgo & Taurus
Leo-Sagittarius & Aries	Aquarius-Libra & Gemini
Virgo-Capricorn & Taurus	Pisces-Cancer & Scorpio

What your Throat chakra friends might say...

***Your wish is my command . . . Be
careful what you wish for***.

Our fifth chakra governs the throat, and rules speech and hearing. This means not only will you find it easy to talk to your Throat chakra friends, but you will also find it natural to listen to them. Lo and behold, these friends are the two signs, other than our own, that we share elements with. Together we form a triangle of knowledge for our element, with Leader, Organizer, and Communicator all meeting up here. Like attracts like, and since we are members of the same element, we are often instantly drawn to these friends. When you start a new job, or move to a new town, these will be some of the first people you meet.

Case Study of Throat Chakra Friendship

This ease of communication with our Throat chakra friends allows us to speak freely about our lives. It is also what enables us to create the things we want around our Throat friends. As a Fire Leader, I have often expressed my wishes freely to Fire Communicators. In return, they have pointed me in the direction I needed to go. When I wanted to leave Halifax as a young woman and try something new for a summer, it was a Fire Communicator who told me about Jasper. "You'll love it," he said. "There are mountains all around and animals walking the streets, tons of people our age, and my sister's friend can get you a job with residence! Do you wanna see some pictures?" Two pages into the photo album I was sold, and then he changed his mind. "On second thought," he said, "I don't really think you should go." "What! Why not?" I asked. "Cuz you'll never come back," he said. I did come home at the end of that summer, but my friend was right: I have been living in Jasper off and on ever since.

It was a Fire Communicator who hired me to work at the restaurant beside the wellness centre where I met my teachers. She further encouraged me to earn my Level 2 Reiki. This Throat chakra friend wasn't even particularly spiritual but through our conversations she learned I was, and so she was inclined to put me on a path.

Once I know where I am going, I have often looked for a Fire Organizer to arrange the details. When I sought redemption for my Spirit after my abortion, it was a Fire Organizer who blessed me with a private Native American prayer ceremony. His compassion helped me forgive myself and move forward with my life.

The challenge of this combination is to be mindful of our words and wishes. It is easy for our element to get out of control with these folks and we must be careful of our tongue. What we speak in words quickly becomes the truth around our Throat chakra friends. Imagine a natural disaster of Earth, Water, Fire, or Air. In these cases we often need other elements to come to the rescue. The same can be said for our Throat chakra friends. Our own element can sometimes overwhelm us and leave us seeking sanctuary from other elements. If we want to make things happen we would be wise to gather around our Throat chakra friends. Just be careful what you ask for because chances are you will get it.

Part 14. Third Eye Chakra
Friendship

Third Eye Chakra Friends at a Glance

Aries-Scorpio & Virgo	Libra-Taurus & Pisces
Taurus-Libra & Sagittarius	Scorpio-Aries & Gemini
Gemini-Scorpio & Capricorn	Sagittarius-Taurus & Cancer
Cancer-Sagittarius & Aquarius	Capricorn-Gemini & Leo
Leo-Capricorn & Pisces	Aquarius-Cancer & Virgo
Virgo-Aquarius & Aries	Pisces-Leo & Libra

What your Third Eye friends might say…

Trust your intuition . . . Trust the facts.

The sixth chakra governs our third eye. Intuition, therefore, often guides us to our Third Eye friends. This makes sense as we do not meet up with these signs as often as the others. Unlike almost all of our other brothers and sisters of the zodiac, we share none of the sun sign traits with this combination. Not only are we far apart on the wheel, which means we are born in different seasons, but we also have uncomplementary elements and hold different jobs as well. Synchronicity often guides us to these folks and we are usually brought together in off-chance or roundabout ways.

Case Study of Third Eye Chakra Friendship

My adoptive father and me are a great example of this connection. I was alive for over a year before I came to his house as a foster child. Another year went by and then I was adopted and he became my father. It was not an automatic relationship: a series of roundabout events lead to its evolution.

One of my oldest Third Eye friends is the one I spoke of in the introduction, the woman I had my first prophetic dream about. Even though we met in elementary school, we were rivals for the first six years of our acquaintance. You see, we liked the same boy, and we used to love to fight over him. It wasn't until we were both geeks in junior high that we decided to join forces. We are often on the opposite side of the playground with these folks in life and yet when the ball happens to roll across the field we are usually in tune with the person kicking it back at us.

The Third Eye chakra is responsible for our psychic abilities. For this reason, we usually have some sort of intuitive connection to our Third Eye friends. Sometimes there can be a telepathic communication between us, where we know when the other is thinking about us, or even what they are thinking about. I have one Third Eye friend who will be waiting at the front door every time I show up unannounced. Or he will already be on the other end of the line when I pick up the phone to call him, only I haven't dialled his number yet. Other times, we share similar interests or abilities related to the psychic realm and great conversations can be had with these signs. In fact, I share the ability to have dreams that come true with a Third Eye friend. Together we have a safe place to talk about things others might consider weird.

It seems as though the two signs that can't find an obvious entrance into our life via location, job, or element have to use subtler methods. They are a representation or reminder of the hidden aspects of ourselves. We all have lunar depths that are not visible in our sun sign. Our Third Eye chakra friends seem to be able to penetrate that shield and tap into our unconscious. The challenge with this combination is that not everyone knows they have a third eye. A lot of my favourite sun sign cynics are Third Eye friends. In these cases, you can get used to hearing "trust the facts." We must remember a balance of fact and feelings is always necessary. Our Third Eye friends can also be here to remind us of that, as perception is formed in the sixth chakra. Be it through fact or intuition, these friends come into our lives to help us see the bigger picture.

Part 15. Crown Chakra Friendship

Crown Chakra Friends at a Glance

Aries-Libra	Libra-Aries
Taurus-Scorpio	Scorpio-Taurus
Gemini-Sagittarius	Sagittarius-Gemini
Cancer-Capricorn	Capricorn-Cancer
Leo-Aquarius	Aquarius-Leo
Virgo-Pisces	Pisces-Virgo

What your Crown chakra friends might say…

Everything happens for a reason…
There is no reason.

The Crown chakra rests on the top of the head. This is our connection to the Divine. In the same way that we only have one earth and therefore only one sun sign that connects to our Root chakra, we have only one Divine, and therefore only one sun sign that connects to our Crown chakra. Our Crown chakra friends are our equal opposites in the zodiac and they sit on the opposite side of the wheel from us. We share jobs with this sign and have elements that blend favourably. In life, we often find these signs at the same place and time as us but for completely different reasons. We share many of the same experiences as our Crown friends, but for different reasons.

Case Study of Crown Chakra Friendship

As the seventh chakra is our spiritual connector, very often these people will encourage our faith. I have had many spiritual associations with my Crown chakra friends. When I was a troubled child, it was a Crown chakra aunt who introduced me to walking in nature. Those moments brought me so much peace and the forest is still my church today. She is the same aunt who gave me my Tarot pack.

Similar spiritual beliefs are often shared, even if we practice our faith differently at times. My sunshine sister, with whom I share an identical tattoo of the sun, is also a Crown connection. She comes from a huge, loving, Catholic family who says grace before each meal and goes to church every Sunday. On the other hand, I was rarely taken to church while growing up, and I have never read the Bible in its entirety. While my friend has a more orthodox background than I do, together we are always able to draw on the beauty found in all faiths. I have gone to church with her and said grace at her family meals. She has walked in nature with me and has always encouraged my fascination for astrology and occult studies.

While this combination is often here to encourage our spirituality, it can also show up to test or prove it. A few years ago, while working in Nova Scotia, a young Crown chakra friend came into the restaurant where I was working to apply for a job. She was incredibly bubbly, and I instantly took a dislike to her. After she dropped off the resume and left, I turned to my manager and said, "There is no reason we should hire this girl."

But she was hired, and before long, to my surprise, we had become friends. One day she asked if I would read her Tarot. When she came over for her reading we ended up talking for hours. Her grandparents were both very sick at the time, and we spoke a lot about Spirit's signs. Not long after, my friend's grandparents both passed, and she moved on from the job at the restaurant. However, we kept in touch.

Three years later, my friend invited my son and me down to her family cottage for the day. It was on a cove, and she explained that, at one time, all of the cottages had belonged to her grandfather and his brothers. It was a beautiful spot, and I was very happy to have this time with my friend, as my family and I were returning to Jasper the following month. As we sat on the beach together, I noticed a turtle in the water. My friend cried, because there used to be hundreds of turtles, and now just seeing one was a miracle. We looked up and watched a bald eagle circling overhead. We felt blessed by our messengers, and planned for one more rendezvous before the big move.

A week before moving back to the mountains, my friend came to visit. She arrived looking astonished. "Oh my god," she said. "I was just talking to my mom at the cottage. Does your biological mom have an older brother?" I answered, "Ah, yeah that's my mom's whole brother. My grandma remarried so my other aunt and uncle have a different father. Why?" She said "Because your uncle is my mother's cousin. So our mothers are actually cousins which means... our grandfathers were brothers!" Spirit reaffirmed itself to me that day. I knew there was indeed a reason for everything.

The challenge of this sign is to learn that the Divine is all encompassing, and not secular. When we judge others or fail to see their reasoning, we are at risk of failing ourselves. If we can respect each other's faith and path, we have much to learn from our Crown chakra friends.

Part 16. How to Apply this Information to Your Own Life

Now that you have finished reading the case studies, I hope you have at least a little curiosity flowing through your veins and an urge to do some detective work. I encourage you to find out what Chakra Sun Signs are in your life and why. There are many benefits to learning this information.

A Common Ground

Perhaps the most simple and yet profound use of this knowledge is finding common ground with every person in your life. Our similarities are often what bind us. The glue that holds any relationship together is usually made up of some sort of shared experience. While these experiences are often hobbies, family, occupation, school, religion, race, or gender, they can also include seasons, elements, sun sign jobs, and chakras.

Whenever you make a connection with another person, be it happy or sad, in love or anger, you are meeting up with them in the same chakra they meet you in.

Remember this before an intimidating job interview. Or quite conversely, remember this when you have one of those rare awkward moments when you are tempted to judge someone else. We all have lessons to teach and learn from one another. With your Chakra Sun Signs, you always meet at a level playing field.

A Confirmation of Spirit

Your Spirit guides you in life, even when you are unaware it exists. When I was writing Chakra Sun Signs I realized through the help of some family and friends that I needed personal case studies to support my theory. As I began to look into my past for stories, I was amazed at how many times my Chakra Sun Signs had guided me without my awareness of them. You may also uncover personal discoveries from your past.

This will require you to reflect on your life, and the milestones you have overcome. Take a look at some of the situations you have been faced with. What chakras did the issues pertain to? Who did you call on, or who was drawn to you in these times? You may become aware of "coincidences" between the issues you were faced with and the friends who were brought forth. You receive what you need from the Universe, even in your hardest lessons.

I hope you are pleasantly surprised when you begin this research. I know it has amazed me at times. It gave me the knowledge that Spirit was always in my life watching out for me.

A Healing Aid

Along with perceiving the past, I encourage you to use this information to access your present. Take a look and recognize how your energy might be useful to someone else. A while back my mother came down with pneumonia. On a day when it was at its worst, my brother and I both called my mom. My brother and I are my mom's Root chakra friends. We all share the same sign. As she was having hallucinations at the time of our calls, I truly believe we were calling to ground her. A Heart chakra friend of my mother's was also compelled to call that day. The energy of this friend aided my mom's heart as well as her lungs.

None of us had realized how sick my mom was until we called. When I spoke to her the following day, she sounded a hundred times better. My mom admitted that after our phone calls, her condition started to improve. In times like this, I think your Spirit steps in. If you feel compelled to call someone, there is probably a good reason for it. Your friend may be calling out for help with a Chakra Sun Sign whistle. Someone needs the energy you have to give, so your Spirit nudges you.

In the same way that you are drawn to give energy to others, your fellow Chakra Sun Sign friends are drawn to give energy to you. For example, if all of a sudden everyone you meet is a certain sign, Spirit may be trying to tell you something. In what chakra does this sign meet up with you? What might they be coming to teach you? Once you know all your combinations with friends and family, you will be more aware when all of your Solar Plexus chakra friends call on the same day. This is an essential message for you. Maybe your Spirit is saying you are in need of a confidence boost, or maybe you are in need of inspiration.

The Colours of Friendship

As you become aware of your own energy, you will be more consciously in touch with which chakras are operating well and which may be over- or underactive. Perhaps you realize your Sacral chakra is underactive, or you have an issue associated with it. You could carry an orange gemstone or eat oranges, as that is the colour associated with this chakra. You could also call on a Sacral chakra friend. In my own experiences, I have found that like attracts like. So if you need a specific chakra friend and can't find one, wear the colour of that particular chakra, and an encounter with a similar energy friend is likely to follow. It's like Batman's signal in the sky. We are all superheroes, you know.

My Reiki master created a chakra cleanse that students were required to complete as part of each Reiki level. This cleanse was an awesome opportunity from which I experienced true growth, and I've continued to do cleanses sporadically ever since. One part of this cleanse involves concentrating on a certain chakra and celebrating the colour associated with it.

On more than several occasions, the chakra and colour I was working with would ultimately generate the energy of those chakra friends. When I was in Root chakra, wearing red, Root chakra friends called. When I was in the Third Eye chakra, wearing indigo, Third Eye chakra friends called. While in the Solar Plexus chakra, wearing yellow, I even got a letter on yellow stationery from a Solar Plexus chakra friend. Similarly, I received a letter in pink from a Heart chakra friend while I was in that chakra and wearing that colour.

Generally, if you have a chakra to heal, you will draw on the appropriate energy to help. However, there are no laws to this, and only your instinct rules. If you are facing an issue that may call for a Crown chakra friend, but you want to call a Throat chakra friend, by all means do so. Your Spirit ultimately knows what you need. Furthermore, your Throat friend may be the one to get you in touch with your Crown friend after all.

A Tool for Understanding

Along with past and present applications to my own life, I have used this information to understand other people and their relationships as well. As an adopted child, understanding my Chakra Sun Signs gives me insight into who my biological parents were as a couple, and what their relationship was based on at the time of my creation. My biological parents connected to each other in the Crown chakra, which tells me they had a spiritual connection. Purple is the colour of the Crown chakra and its number is seven. I chuckle because purple is my favourite colour and seven is my favourite number. This leads me to believe that as a Spirit I was drawn to the energy my parents made together. Somehow I think we all choose our parents before we are born.

It may be interesting for you to take a look and see what chakra your parents connect to each other in.

Adopted or not, this may explain a lot to you. I have done this research with my adoptive parents as well. They connect to each other in the Third Eye chakra, which rules dreams, and psychic abilities. Funny how things work out, isn't it?

Now look at yourself and your siblings; what chakras do each of you meet up with your parents in? Unless everyone in your family has the same sign, you are going to connect at different chakras. This may help you to understand why some people in your family relate in one way while you may do so in another. Another great place to use this tool is at your work, or for evaluating previous relationships. No matter where you are, your energy is constantly changing depending on the person you are interacting with. All Chakra Sun Signs have their own unique purpose and recognizable beauty, and to know them is to love them.

Wish You Were Here

I also believe that your Chakra Sun Signs can act as messengers for someone who cannot be near due to location, circumstance, or death. If you can't find the sign from your own relations when needed, strangers with the same sign will step in to fill the role. They have the same energy to give.

The first time I had this revelation, I was vacuuming the carpet of the restaurant where I worked. "Lady in Red'" by Chris De Burgh was playing on the radio. I remembered that this was the song that was playing in the car the first time my biological father came to visit me. I had a red sweater on that day, and my father sang it to me. I was thirteen years old. Hearing this song on the radio as I vacuumed, I was almost positive it was my father's Spirit saying hello. Then I second-guessed myself, and I thought no, it's just a random song on the radio; if this is really a sign, I'll get another one. Within thirty seconds, the bartender from the pub next door came over to ask me a question. She was a Capricorn, the same sign as my father. I took this as the proof I needed. Spirit is the quiet voice within. We all need to learn how to trust that voice when it speaks.

As a young hippie hitching in the Rockies with my friend, two men stopped to offer us a ride. As a rule, we usually only got in a car with only one driver. However, it was getting late, and we needed to get to our destination, so I asked their signs. They were a Virgo and a Capricorn, the same signs as my dad and biological father. After their answer, we accepted the ride, and arrived safely. I am not suggesting you should try this. To this day however, I am sure my dads' Spirits ordered that safe ride for us.

Natural Resources

If nothing else, I hope this book gives you a renewed sense of purpose, and enables you to see that same value, love, and strength in every person you meet. Too often we judge ourselves by society's standards, and not by the standards of Spirit. How much money we have or do not have, where we live, and what kind of car we drive are false achievements. If we define ourselves by these things, we will almost always lose energy in the long run. Someone will inevitably come along with a nicer car, job, or home, and make us feel like less.

As Chakra Sun Signs, we are all multifarious wonders shining every colour of the rainbow with our various but equal elements. We are many things to many people, and our energy is not only useful, it is also required.

I urge you to use this book as one way of listening to your Spirit. Find out who is in your life and why. Wherever I go, whomever I meet, I ask people what their sign is. I look at this information like stars, guiding my physical and spiritual well-being. Your energy is always leading you to what you need, or where you are needed. Do yourself and the world a favour. Listen.

Afterword. The World

At the end of the Fool's long journey he reaches enlightenment at the World, Tarot card 21. Here all elements operate in balance and harmony. The Fool rests at the heart of all things.

When I began this journey, I truly was a Fool. I did not know where I was going. I did not know why. But I went anyway, and as I travelled I found my way. I hope by the end of this book you are realizing that the world is your Tarot reading, every day, all the time.

When we have a remarkable dream, we are often drawn to a dream book. If we are searching for answers, we often seek readings from a sage. As a society we are obsessed with searching outwardly for answers rather than inwardly. A Tarot reading is a beautiful thing, but not if it makes us think the answers are beyond us. Spirit is always present in our lives and it is always offering the guidance we need. Unfortunately, it is often to the self imposed deaf and blind.

There are times that I worry humanity may lose sight of Spirit altogether. There are so many distractions you see, and Spirit will never pinch sharply, but only tap softy. Society's distractions and expectations are not making Spirit's voice any more audible. In fact, I wonder if there isn't something out there that's afraid of what we might learn. We have cell phones, iPods, laptops, and Twitter. Nobody is looking up anymore, when ideally our Spirit wants our eyes and ears to be open to the energy around us.

We are all searching for ourselves. Stop and look around because we are everyone and everything that we see. In my own Fool's journey to the World I realized that our truth is in all things. We can have our palms read, cast our charts, or have an angel reading. These are all examples of how we try to communicate with Spirit. We can also open up to the World, and in that way our Spirit can speak to us directly. We don't necessarily need a medium, but we need to pay attention to our own details.

Once you have a grasp of this new knowledge, and have gained some enlightenment, you will inevitably become the Fool again. Life is a perpetual cycle. Only this time as a Fool, you will be strengthened with new knowledge. I do not know how this story will end, as I am on the same path myself. I only hope to meet you there.

If any of this rings true in your own life, I am open and eager to hear about your own Chakra Sun Sign stories. Please feel free to write me a letter:

P.O. Box #2697

Jasper, AB

T0E 1E0

or visit me at: chakrasunsigns.com

Selected Bibliography

Andrews, Ted. *The Healer's Manual*. Minnesota: Llewellyn Publications, 2006.

Austin, Jennie. *Practising Reiki*. Scotland: Geddes & Grosset, 1999.

Boushahla, JoJean, and Virginia Reidel-Geubtner. *The Dream Dictionary*. New York:

Berkley Books, 1983.

Goodman, Linda. *Linda Goodman's Love Signs*. New York: Harper Perennial, 1978.

Goodman, Linda. *Linda Goodman's Star Signs*. New York: St Martin's Press, 1988.

Goodman, Linda. *Linda Goodman's Sun Signs*. New York: Bantam, 1971.

Hay, Louise L. *You Can Heal Your Life*. U.S.A.: Hay House, 1984.

Lewis, James R. *The Astrology Book. The Encyclopedia of Heavenly Influences*. Detroit: Visible Ink Press, 2003.

Louis, Anthony. *Tarot Plain and Simple*. Minnesota: Llewellyn Publications, 1996.

Madden, Kristin. *The Book of Shamanic Healing*. Minnesota: Llewellyn Publications,   2002.

Myss, Caroline. *Anatomy of the Spirit*. New York: Three Rivers Press, 1996.

Northrup, Christiane. *Women's Bodies, Women's Wisdom*. New York: Bantam. 1994.

Purna, Svami. *Balanced Yoga*. Rockport: Element Inc., 1992.

Stein, Diane. *Women's Psychic Lives*. Minnesota: Llewellyn Publications, 1995.

Wilde, Claire. *Heal your Soul*. Great Britain: Kyle Cathie Limited, 1995.

Wills, Pauline, and Theo Gimbel. *16 Steps to Health and Energy*. Minnesota: Llewellyn Publications, 1992.

Thank You

Fleurette Knaggs, Stephanie Jollymore, Billie Ann Whalen, Kira Doyle, 'Budda' Wells, Angela Hardman, Zach S., Kay S., Marianne Garrah, Beth Le Blanc, Alison Barrett, Sharon Whitman, Leslie Marion, Cheryl Grant, Jose Hull, Stacey Greenough, James Cross, Deanna Perry, Joan Faulds, Leonard Oakley, Christopher Constantine, Stephen Langille, Kenny MacClean, Diane Marquis, LeeAnn Marion, Kim Haas, Dieter, Leanne Stanko, Kelty Moser, Angela Bolton, Maggie Mac, Nancy Addison, Patty Moore, Jim Baldwin, Mary Horwell, George Greene, Shawn Oliver, Mick Meagher, Anthony Cooper, Scott Urbanovitch, Jason Maure, Nicolas Pilon, Dayna Mickelson, Leslie Chernecki, Laurie McWhinnie, John Clark, Janis Kilgar, Richard H, Alanna Downie, Marcy Cariou, Koren Beaman, Kelly Hoytt, Pam Andrew, Tully, Laura James, Jack Lawson, Irene Bryden, Kenny Hiles, Charlie Hiles, Andrew Oliver, Margaret Meagher, Mike Spurr, Allison Barker, Andrew Box, Cathy Neil, Christine Oeggerli, Big John Glaves, Peter Lynch, Oliver Andrew, Jill Corman, Angela Mather, Janet Barker, Helen Mills, Stepha Andrew, Mittens, Janet Woods, Jen MacBride, Jordan Mitchell, Ann and John Oliver, Kevin Sullivan, Art and Val Knaggs, Pat Greene, Jay Meister, Aprile Swartz, Brandy Bayda, Joanne Andrew, Hannah Gibson, Sarah Dion, Amy Labolt, Jacyln Marquis, Teeny, Aaron Byers, Jack Woods, Tim Lindsay, Helen Cross, Apollo Hardman, Michael Cross, Evelynn Greene, Lynwood Bryden, Troix Cook, San Fung, Mark Bowie, Robert J'reige, Melissa Cresswell, Robert McClean, Arlene Gillard

Brief Bio of the Author

Born on April 7, 1974, in Nova Scotia, Canada, Santina Cross is a spiritualist and freelance writer who began her independent study of the occult after a series of prophetic dreams about others in the mid-nineties.

Her research involves many areas of spirituality, including martial arts, dream work, tarot, numerology, astrology, totems, colour energy, Reiki, yoga, and the

photo by Jim Baldwin

chakra system. Her studies are complemented with a degree in English from Dalhousie University, and a deep love of people and travel. These pursuits have enabled Santina to learn, counsel, and inspire the universal public for almost twenty years.

As a spiritualist, Santina has found her discovery of the Chakra Sun Signs to be as significant and valuable to her own life as it is to those seeking her advice. The desire to share this information with others compelled her to write *Chakra Sun Signs* and to create a workshop based on the theory. She recently held her eighth successful workshop and has more booked for the winter of 2014.

Santina Cross loves, writes, and converses with Spirit in Jasper, Alberta, Canada where she lives in the mountains with her boyfriend, Cory, their son, Apollo and their lovable pets, Tully the dog and Mittens the kitten.

Brief Bio of the Illustrator

Marla Joy Pollock grew up in the Lower Fraser Valley of British Columbia. After graduating from Chilliwack High School in 1984, she completed her foundation year at Nova Scotia College of Art and Design in Halifax, Nova Scotia. She spent a second

year studying printmaking at Emily Carr College in Vancouver.

In 1989 she travelled and settled in Alberta, and finally took up painting after being hired on as a gallery attendant at Sunrise Gallery in Jasper. Sunrise Gallery

helped launch Jasper's Artist Guild, which has represented Marla ever since.

Marla's work is infused with bold line and colour.
Semi-representational, they are journalistic storylines
of her current state of being. Her art also reflects the
energy of events surrounding her, both personal and
beyond.

Art is a very healing, meditative endeavour for Marla.
She believes that risking the journey without a creative outlet is like trying to resist breathing!

CPSIA information can be obtained
at www.ICGtesting.com
Printed in the USA
LVHW071958141119
637425LV00002B/5/P

* 9 7 8 0 9 9 4 0 0 5 8 9 2 *